# Narcissistic Personality Disorder Guide 2021

*Recovery with an Emotional Guide from Epidemic Narcissism in Relationship, Workplace and Life.*

# Table of Contents

validity or interim quality. Trademarks that are mentioned are done without written consent and can in no way be considered an endorsement from the trademark holder.

# Introduction

The following chapters will discuss all the things that you need to know in order to fully understand narcissism, and what Narcissistic Personality Disorder, or NPD, is all about. Dealing with a narcissist can be hard. These individuals often only want a lot of attention and focus on them, and their empathy is going to be pretty low. When this all comes together, it can be hard to work with them or understand how to get along with them without getting hurt in the process.

This guidebook is going to take some time to look at NPD and narcissism and some of the things that you can do when these things strike. We will start out with a look at the basics of NPD, the symptoms and behaviors of NPD, and how to understand a bit more about what a narcissist is. From there, we will look at what leads to narcissism and some of the research that has been done in that area.

Next, we will spend some time looking at the various treatments that are out there. While these are not automatically going to be fixed with treatment, and not all of them are going to work, treatment is able to help some of those who are dealing with NPD and who are considered narcissists. We will explore what will happen when someone with NPD doesn't get treatment and some of the best treatments when it comes to dealing with NPD.

From there, we are going to spend a bit more time looking at some more of the things you need to know when it comes to NPD and narcissism. We will look at some of the myths of NPD, how to ask for help if you are currently dealing with NPD and a narcissist, how to understand megalomania, narcissism, and depression, and how to handle your interactions with a narcissist.

Narcissism can be a hard thing to deal with. When someone you love and trust is a narcissist, you want to be there for them, but often, the interactions that you have with them make this really hard. When you are ready to learn a bit more about narcissism and NPD, and how to handle both of these, make sure to read through this guidebook to help you get started.

There are plenty of books on this subject on the market. Thanks again for choosing this one! Every effort was made to ensure it is full of as much useful information as possible, please enjoy!

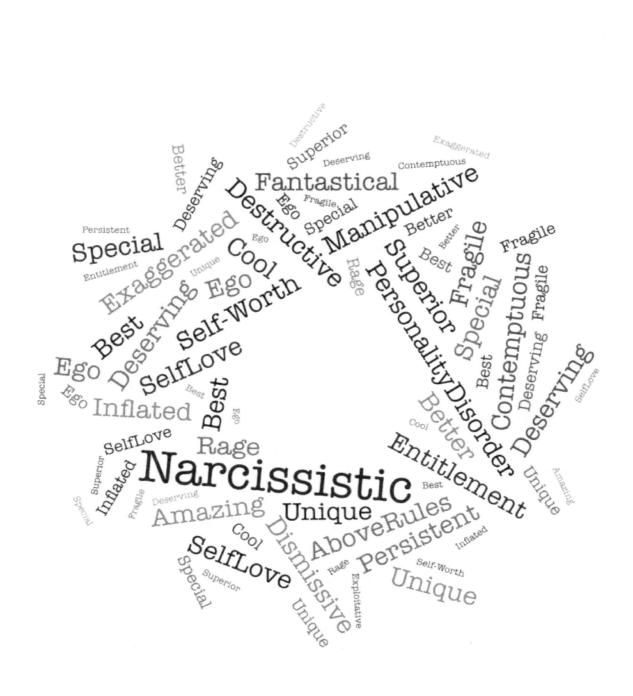

# Chapter 1: The Basics of Narcissistic Personality Disorder

Before we are able to fully understand what NPD or Narcissistic Personality Disorder is all about, we need to get a better look at what narcissism is all about. This word comes from the Greek myth of Echo and Narcissus Echo who is known as a wood nymph who fell in love with a man who was very beautiful, and also very vain. His name was Narcissus. This man ignored the wood nymph and she ended up dying by a broken heart.

At the time, the gods took pity on poor Echo, and they were very angry about the pride and the vanity that Narcissus was showing. They decided that, as a punishment, he needed to live alone, and that he would never know the love of another human. One day, while Narcissus was bending down into some water to get a drink, he found that he fell in love with his own reflection. He decided to never leave it and died beside that pool.

It wasn't until 1898 that the British psychologist Havelock Ellis started to use this story to help him describe what is known as a pathological self-absorption. It wasn't long until others in the field started to pick up these terms as well and this is when we started hearing about being narcissistic and narcissist. The words soon came into everyday use after Sigmund Freud wrote a paper about it, and introduced the phenomenon to the whole world.

# Are there different expressions of NPD?

Now that we know a bit about the background of narcissism and where it comes from, it is time to take this to the next level. What exactly is narcissism? As with the boy in the myth, there is going to be a kind of obsession with oneself when you suffer from narcissism. But when we describe this, there is going to be a lot more to it rather than just high self-esteem, or conceited, or egotistical, or even full of oneself. Of course, all of these can be problems as well and can cause some issues in a relationship, but they are not really the full definition of narcissism.

True narcissism is going to be much more than this. You will find that it is going to be an ego that is incredibly pumped up, as well as an almost maniacal pursuit of ambition, praise, and gratification.

For those who have any degree of this NPD, there is going to be a certain level of being arrogant, smug, and vain. And many of them are going to appear to have a self-esteem that is much higher than normal. But, for the most part, narcissists, at least on the inside, are going to seem like they are insecure, and like they don't feel their self-worth is very high. They are going to feed their belief in their own importance from the admiration that they are able to get from others

This is something that is known as the narcissistic supply. For a drug, this supply is as potent as the supply of drugs that someone could get when they become an addict. Narcissists are going to be addicted to a need for confirmation of their belief in their own superiority. They will often also come with a lack of empathy, which means in addition to needing all of this praise and affirmation from others; they are not going to really care about the feelings of those around them

As with any condition, there are going to be several different levels that come with narcissism, which is why it is sometimes hard to figure out whether you are dealing with a narcissist or not. In fact, some experts will agree that all of us are going to come with a bit of narcissism in us. However, for the use of this guidebook, there are a few criteria that need to be met before someone can be given the diagnosis of NPD. These symptoms will include:

1. The individual is not able to put things into the right perspective. In many cases, they will take a certain situation and blow it way out of proportion.
2. The narcissist is going to have little to no empathy with others, and they find that identifying with the thoughts or feelings of another person is almost impossible.
3. They will not care about the problems of others. This is partly because they don't care at all, and partly because they are too busy thinking about their own problems.
4. This person is going to decide that authority is not worth their respect at all. And they have little concern when it comes to morals.
5. This person is going to have a lot of feelings of inferiority. Because of this, they are going to try to make things change so that they can feel like they are the superior one in any given situation.
6. The person is going to be really sensitive to any criticism that they receive. While they have no problem with giving out criticism to

others if they think that it is necessary, if you give them any criticism, it is going to be a horrible thing.

7. The narcissist can often be an exhibitionist and they like to have admiration that is sexual.
8. These individuals are not able to make it on their own and need other people to give them attention and to help them with silly things. They are also vain and they like to exploit any person or situation that they can.

All of the cases of NPD will show these traits to some extent. But you will also find that there are a few different types of narcissists that you will need to be aware of. Since the 1950s, there has been a dramatic increase in the number of people who are diagnosed as a narcissist. And as these numbers increase, it is easier for the therapists to start noticing that there are differences in the narcissists they treat.

The first way that therapists decided to split up this group of people was by age. This was done because a lot of the tendencies for this issue in children will be more of learned behavior. If the tendency was caught at an early enough stage, then it was likely that it could be unlearned. At the time, it was believed that the full-blown version of NPD could only exist in adults, and because of this, they needed to be treated in a different manner.

While there isn't really an agreement on how to split up this personality type yet, there are a few types of narcissists that we can focus on in this chapter to help us better understand what is going on. Some of the different types of narcissism that you should be aware of include:

1. The craving narcissist: Despite the inflated ego that is common in NPD, craving narcissists are going to be really needy, and maybe clingy to others emotionally. They may demand love and attention from all of those around them.

2. The paranoid narcissist: These are going to be the opposite of what we just talked about above. These are going to inwardly be paranoid and will have a lot of self-loathing with them. This is then going to be projected outward as extreme sensitivity to criticism and almost maniacal jealousy.

3. The manipulative narcissist: This is going to be the narcissist who most likely knows who they are, and they find that it is very enjoyable to manipulate and influence those around them. The manipulative narcissist is going to feed the need they have for power by intimidating others. And to do this, they may resort to using tricks like manipulation, lies, and bullying.

4. The phallic narcissist: Those who fall into this group are usually males, but they can include some females on occasion. These people are not only in love with themselves but also with their body image. You will find that they are exhibitionists who like to show off their clothes, muscles, and anything else that shows how manly they are. They will often be athletic and aggressive as well.

One thing that you will notice with all of the narcissistic personality types is that there is a lot of grandiosity. This is not the same thing as regular boasting or being prideful. Instead, it is going to imply a level of self-aggrandizement that is going to have little to no basis in reality at all. If a person goes on and on about being the MVP of basketball back in college, it may be a bit of conceit or ill-mannered boasting. It is annoying, but it is not something to worry about.

On the other hand, if you are talking to someone who talks on and on about being the MVP of the basketball team in college, when they just sat on the bench, or they never actually went to college, then this is them being grandiose, and it could be a sign of narcissism as well.

# Millon's Subtypes

To take this a bit further, there are a few other subtypes that are recognized when it comes to the narcissistic personality. Theodore Millon, a psychotherapist in America, is well-known for his groundbreaking work that allowed him to really identify a whole host of personality disorders. During his time doing this, he came up with a few additional subtypes of narcissism that we should take a look at. These include:

1. The unprincipled narcissist: This type is going to include a lot of pathological lying, as well as a deliberate deception in order to obtain that narcissistic supply that we talked about earlier. The person who fits into this section is going to be unscrupulous, deceptive, abusive, and a con man.
2. The amorous narcissist: This person is going to have a type of obsession about seduction and erotica. They will use sex and sex appeal as their own tool, and even a weapon in order to get the power and the control that they want. This doesn't just stop with people of the opposite sex; this person has no problems using their charisma on those on the other sex as well.
3. The compensatory narcissist: This one is going to use the narcissistic supply in order to compensate for their feelings of low self-esteem and inadequacy. They like to work to make an illusion of being

superior to others and to create a good image of high self-worth.

4. The elitist narcissist: This kind of narcissist is going to have the same characteristics that we talked about earlier with the phallic narcissist, but it isn't exclusively male.

5. The fanatic narcissist: These individuals are going to come with the belief that they are gods on earth, but they have a lot of paranoia as well. They are going to work on fighting their poor self-esteem with a lot of delusions of grandeur along the way.

## Abusing drugs and alcohol

Because these narcissists are going to be, by nature, dependent, they are often going to face issues with drug and alcohol abuse. These individuals are going to be dependent on almost everything. They are going to depend on others to feed this inflated view of themselves. They are going to crave idolization by others just like a physical addiction. Because of all this dependency, it is not that surprising to find out that narcissists are also going to become dependent on other things. Many times, you will find that a narcissist is going to also fall into some other dependencies including drug addiction, alcoholism, workaholism, compulsive shopping, and more.

The narcissist, just like with other addicts, is going to get a lot of pleasure from the actions and the behaviors that are able to feed this narcissistic supply. When this ends up falling short, they are going to turn to some other sources to help them out, to help them get their high, such as alcohol, drugs, and sex.

Both alcohol and drugs are able to give you pleasure and will be able to provide anyone, whether they are a narcissist or not, a way to get away from the pressures of reality. Those who suffer from NPD will decide to take drugs and to drink in order to help them support that super inflated self-image that they have been holding onto for all of this time.

In addition, any kind of risky or dangerous behavior can be something that the narcissist is more likely to do. It allows them to feel like they are in control over something, even if they aren't, and so they will continue to do it. It can also help them to keep up that grandiose outlook of themselves,

something that they may not be able to do on their own, and they may not be able to find others to do for them.

While we are on this topic, eating disorders are going to be closely linked to tendencies of a narcissist. People who are suffering from the various eating disorders out there are going to be obsessed with body image. Narcissists are going to be reckless as well as impulsive, and they can easily develop one of these eating disorders because of the same reasons that they will become drug abusers or alcoholics. Their desire to exert power or influence over some aspect of their lives pushes them towards doing this.

# Relationship issues

The last thing that we are going to take a look at here is going to be that of relationship issues. In the worldview of a narcissist, all of the relationships that they could have are going to be doomed from the start. This strong belief is going to come, in many cases, from some kind of early trauma during their childhood, or some other negative experience that caused them to feel abandoned, betrayed, or humiliated.

Even though this is a belief that was formed, for one reason or another, many years ago, to the narcissist, any interaction that is emotional or any connection that is going to need a commitment that is emotional, has to end badly. This means that getting attached to anything, even an idea, a job, a person, a career, or a home, is a horrible thing. This is one of the reasons that you will find narcissists will work to avoid any kind of intimacy.

Of course, they do need to have people around them most of the time. Otherwise, it would be impossible for the narcissist to feed their supply. But even with a bunch of people around them, the narcissist is not able to make any real friendships, or truly love others, or express any real feelings of attachment or commitment.

On the other side of things, it is going to be really hard for you to be in a relationship with someone who is a narcissist. You will find that this person is going to live in a bubble, one that only allows them to see their own reflection. It doesn't really matter how hard you try to enter the bubble, you are not able to get in. And this can lead you to feel frustrated, hurt, and alone.

It doesn't matter what kind of relationship is there. The narcissist is unable to develop any pleasure from the relationship, and they are not going to develop any good sense of security either. The only thing that a narcissist is willing to invest emotionally in is going to be themselves.

Dealing with a narcissist can be a challenge. We will explore this some more as we go through this guidebook. But since the narcissist just wants to have others around to build them up, and they are not really interested in how that makes others feel, it is hard to form a good relationship with someone who is a narcissist. Working to gain a better understanding of what a narcissist is, and how you can work with them in real life, can make the best sense for making this work.

# Chapter 2: The Symptoms and Behaviors of NPD

To start this chapter, we are going to take a look back. Remember when your child had reached the terrible twos? Remember the tantrums, the yelling, and the demands? Of course, while that year or so may have been hard on the parents, it is a time period that our children grew out of. But not when it comes to a narcissist. These individuals are usually going to be stuck there, even when they are all grown up. And these kinds of bad behaviors, the destructive ones, are going to be left so that those around them have to deal with it.

With that in mind, let's take a look at some of the symptoms, and some of the behaviors that can come with NPD.

## Causes and risk factors

As with any of the other emotional disorders that you may study, there is not going to be one cause that will start NPD. But, just as there is a chance that you can catch a cold if you run around in short sleeves and pants on a cold and rainy day, there are some factors that can increase your risk for developing any behavior that would be considered narcissistic.

Along with many of the other mental illnesses out there, the roots of NPD are going to be complex. The likelihood of developing this issue is often linked to events during childhood, as well as with parenting that is dysfunctional. One thing that is interesting here is that too much pampering, as well as abuse and neglect, are both going to be associated with NPD developing and with these tendencies of narcissism. Recent thinking has also been able to point to genetics and the connection between the brain of the person and their behavior.

Another thing to look at is that, statistically, more men than women are going to suffer from this disorder. And for the most part, although there are some exceptions to this, NPD is not going to show up in children. But the experts are taking time to look more into this condition and to see if they are better able to pinpoint what may be causing it.

While there is a lot of unknown when it comes to this condition, there are a few risk factors that could make it more likely for the individual to develop this disorder. These include:

1. Parents that end up ignoring the needs and fears of the children.

2. Parents who belittle the fears of the child, or those who say that they are signs of weakness, especially in male children.
3. A general lack of affection, as well as a lack of positive praise during childhood.
4. Neglect, as well as any other form of emotional abuse that occurred in childhood.
5. Parents who gave unreliable or inconsistent care during childhood.
6. Imitation of manipulative behaviors that they learned from their parents.

Children, especially when it comes to male children, are going to be made to believe in many instances, and this usually happens by the father, that to show any kind of vulnerability is unmanly and unacceptable. When this happens too often, the child is going to start losing their compassion and empathy for others. In order to become more superhero-like in the eyes of their father, these children are going to start covering up any of their emotional needs, rather than showing them. The covers are sometimes going to include egotistical and grandiose behaviors that ensure that the child is going to be protected against the emotions. And these coverup behaviors are going to lead to NPD later in life.

# The red flags of NPD

People who develop this disorder are often going to appear, to the outside world, as having an overinflated sense of their own importance, and an overwhelming hunger for the admiration and the approval of those around them. When they show little, and often no, regard for the feelings of others, it can help them to believe in their own superiority more. But buried under this skin of confidence is going to be someone who is fragile, someone who is going to have a lot of trouble accepting any criticism that is thrown at them.

If you don't know about narcissism that much in the beginning, it may seem like the most important characteristics of this disorder are as simple as being strong-willed, having too much confidence, or having a strong sense of self-esteem. But when we are looking at NPD, we have crossed the line here. It is more about going down a darker path, one where the person thinks so highly of themselves that they have put themselves on a pedestal while believing that others are beneath them. In comparison, those who just have a healthy amount of self-confidence are not going to need to build themselves up by breaking down others.

With all of this information, you can see that it is not always an easy thing to recognize who is a narcissist and who just has a lot of self-confidence. Because of their nature, these narcissists are going to be masters of deceit and disguise. They are able to hide themselves behind a mask of false self-image.

Now, there is a lot of debate out there about what is going to be full-blown NPD. But some of the behaviors that you can look for to try and determine if someone is dealing with NPD or not include:

1. Does the other person try to make sure that you are cut off from others including relatives and friends? Or do they at least try to limit how much you can be in contact with these people?
2. Is the other person really jealous? Do they invent a relationship out of thin air and then will suspect that you are not faithful with those you know, including with coworkers and friends?
3. Is the other person belittling when they talk to you?
4. Does the other person have to resort to physical or verbal abuse to get what they want?
5. Are there any times when the other person is going to try and punish you for what you have done, even if it seems like you did nothing?
6. Has there been a time when the other person has withdrawn from you emotionally?
7. How well does the other person admit to being wrong? Have they ever been able to admit when they were wrong?
8. Does this person try to control your time?
9. When you are with this person, are there ever any issues about them trying to threaten you or intimidate you?
10. Does this person ever go through and try to purposely destroy things that are yours?
11. Have you ever had this person claim that they know your motivations and feelings better than you do?

# Understanding your own sense of self

Another way that you are able to tell if you are living with a narcissist or not is to look at the behaviors that you have as well. Think about the way that you feel. Do you change the behavior that you have when your partner is nearby, do you ever let your guard down (or how often is it up), or do you feel like you are constantly walking on eggshells and that this relationship is always one-sided?

Be honest with yourself when you are doing this. Often, we have become so used to the behavior and how it makes us feel, that we don't even stop to think about what it is actually doing to us. You need to take a good hard look at yourself. Do you like what you see there? Do you feel like the same person you were when you first got started with this relationship? If you are not happy with the answers that you are giving here, then it is time to make some changes

Now, if you have been living with the narcissist for long enough, it is going to be even harder to recognize what is going on. You may start to believe the belittling that they do, and you may begin to develop feelings of inadequacy. This is sometimes going to occur without us really knowing what is going on. Many times, the victim is going to come into the relationship feeling pretty good about themselves and having a fairly decent self-image. But once they spend a good amount of time with the narcissist, then this is going to fade away as well.

Narcissists are going to love it when they can play the blame game. These individuals are going to end up internalizing their failure, and their first reaction to the failure of any kind is to feel shame, rather than determination to improve, responsibility, or guilt. Shame is something that the narcissist needs to avoid as much as possible, so they are going to find a way that someone else can be blamed for the failure, no matter what it is.

These people are going to get it in their heads that there is no way that the problem could be their fault, or there is no way that they could have failed. The blame lies with someone else, someone who should have done the work, someone who should have helped them, and someone who just dropped the ball. When it comes to the narcissist, nothing is ever their fault.

A change in your own self-image can also lead to another powerful emotion that you will feel when you are near the partner with NPD which is fear. Think about how you feel when you are around your partner. It is likely that you feel some level of fear when you are around them, or like you need to watch all of your moves, where you need to refuse to be yourself, and where you may be worried about upsetting them all the time.

## The symptoms

Now that we have taken a moment to look at the cause of NPD, and how the individual who is living with someone who has NPD may feel, it is time to look at some of the symptoms. The words of Narcissism and Narcissistic have been going around our modern world for some time, but this has brought up a level of confusion because not everyone knows the true meaning or the symptoms that they need to watch out for.

When we meet someone who has NPD, they are often going to come across as arrogant, egotistical, and conceited. These are the people who are willing and able to take over the conversation, belittle others, look down on the ones around them, and look for others to help them inflate their ego a bit more.

You may find that this kind of individual is going to walk around with feelings of entitlement. There are times when they are going to be described as being emotionally immature. When they feel that they are entitled to something, and then they don't get it, they are going to revert back to their two-year-old self and throw tantrums, give the silent treatment, and make the other person feel miserable for saying no.

There are a few general behaviors that you can watch out for when it comes to someone who has NPD. These will include:

1. If someone believes that they are better than everyone else, even without a good reason for thinking this way, then they are possibly a narcissist.

2. If this person likes to fantasize about being in power and having a lot of success, they may be a narcissist.
3. If this person likes to lie or exaggerate about their own talents or achievements, then it is likely they are a narcissist.
4. If this person demands a constant amount of admiration and praise, then they may be a narcissist.
5. If this person believes that they are special, or like they are beyond any legal or moral consequences, then they might be a narcissist.
6. If this person fails to recognize that others have feelings, then it is likely they are a narcissist.
7. If this person expects that others are always going to be happy and willing to go along with their plans and ideas, then they are a narcissist.
8. If this person enjoys the fact that they can manipulate or take advantage of those around them, then they are a narcissist.

9. If this person always shows that they are jealous of others, while still thinking that others are more jealous of them, they are a narcissist.

10.      If this person likes to set goals that are completely unrealistic, then they might be a narcissist.

11.      If the person thinks that showing emotions is going to be a sign of weakness, then they may be a narcissist.

Most narcissists are only going to put their emotional investment into one thing, and one thing only; their false self-image. If a narcissist seems like they value another person, it is usually because they think that person has something to offer or some way to feed the narcissistic supply. People are just useful tools in life, and nothing more. But it is still unlikely that the narcissist is actually going to care for that other person. In fact, it is likely

that this individual, even though they seem to hold value to the narcissist on the outside, is going to be the one who gets the worst out of the narcissist's cruel attitude and mistreatment.

And one more thing that you can do to spot a narcissist? Trust that gut feeling. There may not be a good way to explain the feeling, but when you are dealing with a narcissist, it may be a matter of knowing one when you see them. Maybe you feel uneasy when you are near them, even if there isn't a good reason for this. Or there just seems to be something off with that person. Trusting your gut is a great way for you to avoid dealing with a narcissist.

# Chapter 3: Understanding the Narcissist

At this point, we are going to take a closer look at who are narcissists, and how you are able to spot these kinds of behaviors. The question that a lot of people have is how they know whether they are a narcissist or not. Therapists might respond to that question with something like "if you have to ask the question, then it is highly unlikely that you are a narcissist. Narcissists aren't likely to think that there is any problem with them, and so they would never think in this way."

But there are some things that you can look for when you are trying to spot a narcissist. Remember, these people want to find others who are able and willing to feed into the over-inflated ego and sense of self. They will often have trouble even understanding what emotions are and definitely won't care about what others feel at all. If you don't feel these things, then it means that you are not a narcissist.

Most experts are going to agree that there are nine areas that the behavior of narcissism will cover. As you read the list, you may notice that one or two of them may be able to describe you. But this is because all of us have a few narcissistic tendencies that we are dealing with. But, a true narcissist is going to feel most, if not all, of these characteristics and areas. The nine areas of narcissistic behavior that you should be aware of include:

1. A manner that is grandiose and likes to be exaggerated. They feel that they have no flaws or failures, and they think that they are much more important than they really are.

2. A preoccupation with fantasies that they can reach an unlimited amount of beauty, perfect love, brilliance, power, and success.
3. They are convinced of being really unique or special, even though they don't really have a good reason to believe this.
4. They always need to have some special admiration from those around them
5. They think that they are entitled to having special treatment all the time. And they think that others need to comply with these expectations.
6. Taking advantage of others for one's own purpose, without any care of how it is going to affect others.
7. Feeling an intense amount of jealousy of others and believing others who are envious of them.
8. Arrogant and haughty.
9. A lack of empathy, or feeling, for the needs of others, no matter how close they are together.

Even when we look through these categories, there is going to be a wide range of what would be considered the behavior of narcissism, from mild to the severe form of this personality disorder. The level that the individual is dealing with can depend on how many of these behaviors the person is going to demonstrate on a regular basis. Five or more of these traits happening on a consistent basis could indicate that the person is dealing with a narcissistic personality disorder.

# The risk factors

Now that we know a bit more about narcissism and what it stands for, there are a number of risk factors that can make a difference in whether someone is likely to develop this disorder. While there are some risk factors present, it is important to note that just having one or more of these factors in your life doesn't guarantee that the person is going to come up with this disorder. Some of the risk factors that come with NPD include:

*Parenting*

There is usually something that occurred in the childhood of the individual who suffers from NPD. There is a wide range with this one, ranging from over-indulgence of the child to child neglect. These theories could include things like the parent not giving enough praise and affection during childhood, but too much can be a problem as well. Many times, unreliable parenting (sometimes, this is on purpose, and sometimes, it could be while the parent is dealing with an illness or another issue), neglect and emotional abuse, and a parental lack of comforting and understanding. If the parent shows a lot of manipulative behaviors, then the child may learn them as well.

*The role of our culture*

There are some social learning theorists who will argue that many of the trends that are found in our society are going to contribute to the risks of this disorder. There are a number of these cultural trends that can influence this disorder. First, the idea that the media centers on celebrities, rather than average people, can cause issues. There is a lot of importance that is placed on achievements and status. There is more of an acceptance and a choosing of leaders with an emphasis on their appearance and personality. And to add to all of this, there seems to be a weakening of many social and religious institutions that helped to encourage community, rather than individuality.

All of these can come together and make it more likely that others will start to develop this disorder. Social researchers are going to describe this as a kind of acquired situational narcissism. They believe that this is able to affect many adults as a result of social successes.

*Genetics*

There is also some new research that shows how there could be a genetic basis for personality disorders including NPD. One evidence with this has been with identical twins who were separated at birth, but they were still able to maintain some similar personality traits, even though they lived with different families and were exposed to different social situations throughout the years.

Thanks to some new technology on brain scanning, it is now possible to document abnormal brain functions or even some of the problems that show up in the brain of those with certain personality disorders. Research has found that at least 68 percent of children who have parents with a personality disorder is also going to suffer the same disorder as their parents.

For example, about two-thirds of the children who had parents with NPD would then be diagnosed with NPD as well. But even with this research, there are two questions that need to be solved through here. First, there needs to be more research to figure out if there is a genetic predisposition to these personality disorders, or do they develop if there is a trigger in childhood, such as some type of trauma. Or could the disorder be genetic and it doesn't need a trigger before it starts to show itself.

## Are some people more likely to suffer from this disorder?

The data that has come in from clinicians, researchers, and hospitals on the percentage of the general population with NPD is going to vary from less than one percent to 6.2 percent. However, it is common to see this more in men compared to women. Statistics show that at least 50 percent, though sometimes, as high as 75 percent, of those diagnosed with this disorder are going to be men.

The reason for this could be in the way that boys and girls will deal with criticism. Girls are more likely to take that criticism and internalize it, but boys are more likely to act out as their response to it. One explanation for why this happens could be in the way the brand functions for girls and boys. This difference can explain, at least in part, the traditional behavior roles of males and females as well.

If the role of the female is to nurture, it is more likely that women are going to give up their narcissism in order to tend to the needs of someone else. Because of this, the female is less likely to suffer from NPD than a man. This doesn't mean that she will never have to deal with this issue; it simply means that it is less likely. It is possible that learned behavior, which can be reinforced by societal expectations and more, can mean that even women may deal with this disorder as well.

## Can a narcissist live a life that is normal?

Therapists, no matter which level they are going to practice at, would come to the agreement that someone with NPD would have an impaired capacity to be interested in, or to love, others. This can be found in those who have more mild behaviors of a narcissist. However, many of the therapists who are working on treating this disorder have some encouragement to offer when it comes to living with someone who has this disorder.

For example, there are therapists who will discuss some of the narcissists that they have been able to counsel, and some of the difficulties that can show up with them leading a life that would be considered. Of course, on the surface, the narcissist looks like they are leading very functional lives. They are able to hold jobs and many even marry and have a family.

But, when we look at these professional and personal areas, narcissists can experience some problems. They may use sex as their substitute for intimacy and love. They have an intense fear of intimacy because it does leave them feeling exposed. Plus, to have intimacy with another person, you need to have some sort of empathy for the feelings and needs of another person, which they just can't make themselves do. Many times a relationship is going to end because of the grandiosity of the narcissist, or because the other partner feels alone because of the detachment that is there.

When it comes to their jobs, a narcissist is able to hold onto a good job, and sometimes, they are able to do well, but they just can't have contact with their coworkers outside of work hours. But there could be issues, especially when it comes to the boss and being too grandiose.

In these cases, it is best if the individual is able to do some therapy. This helps them to get more in touch with the real feelings they have, the ones that are buried down deep in many cases. This makes it easier for them to start understanding how others feel and can make it easier for them to get along with others, to have healthier and happier relationships, and to stop some of the issues that may be creeping into their marriages or relationships, and even at work.

# Chapter 4: What Leads to Narcissism?

How do people start becoming narcissists? There are several theories and a lot of research that will point to a combination of psychobiology and genetics, which is basically the connection between the brain, thinking, and behavior. However, psychologists often believe that biology is just going to be one of the forces that can shape adults. They often believe that parenting, society, and culture are going to be more important.

With all of these different things that can shape who we are, it is hard to know which things we can control and stop the start of narcissism and how you can prevent it from happening. Let's take a look at some of the different things that can influence narcissism.

## The brain and its plasticity

The good news here is that research shows how the brain does have a lot of plasticities. The nerves and our brain are not rigid, so even our personality traits are not going to be carved into stone. There are things that can cause some emotional scars to the brain, including abuse and trauma. But there is always going to be a window of plasticity. During that time, you can do some fixing to the damage like love, care, compassion, and empathetic experiences. The issue here is that a lot of people have no idea how long the window is open. It could be a few years, and it could be decades.

Even with this idea, there are still many other possibilities of how narcissism can take control because it becomes a personality or a behavior:

1. According to a few theories, a person is going to be born with a certain personality, and they will meet with all of the experiences that

occur in their life in a particular way, all due to what they are born with.

2. There are other theories that suggest that the interactions and the roles of parenting and other caregivers are going to mark and influence the development of personality in a child. These theories are going to note the role of the mother, who is going to help shape the feelings of self in the child.

3. Some theories are going to contend that the personality that is inside the child will allow this child to adapt to different situations in their own way. But then, it can be flipped the other way. This one states that situations the child encounters will determine the personality of the child.

4. Many of the theories that come out will point to neglect or abuse that may be beyond the parents' control.

5. In more recent times, theorists have discussed the influence of the media, lifestyle, pressures, socialization, and culture on the development of a personality, even as the person gets on in age.

As you start to read through a lot of the different possibilities that can influence the personality and can start the development of narcissism in the individual, you will probably start to think about how you developed as a child, and whether or not you had the potential to become a narcissist at some point. In any way, this is going to be able to help you understand more about the challenges you may face when you are dealing with someone who has NPD.

# Child abuse

Child abuse is one of the first things that theorists will look at when they meet with someone who has NPD. When we look at the term of abuse, it leads us to think about physical abuse, sexual perversions, or neglect of water, food, comfort, and sleep. But it is also possible, in this situation as well, that the child abuse will also contain a lack of attention and catering to a child's emotional needs as abusive.

Sometimes, these situations are going to be on purpose, meaning that the parent wanted to cause harm to the child. Then there are times when it is unintentional, such as when the parent is dealing with physical challenges, medical challenges, financial challenges, and more. Whether it was on purpose or not, any of these can be like violence to the child.

As a response to the abuse that they are dealing with, the developing child may end up developing some repressed emotions or some denial of reality. They could strike out in anger or some physical violence. And sometimes, they are going to end up in their own world, one with a lot of fantasy, where they are able to find the security and love that they need, where they find they are good and perfect.

# The role of image

There is also a theory that the emotional development of a child is going to be based on the image that they will form of themselves, in their own heads. They will usually start to develop a healthy and positive image from loving and sensitively-caring parents. But if you end up with a parent who is cold or one who struggles with being empathetic to their child, it is common that the child is going to feel hurt and will start to look for some safety inside their own head.

Because of this, the child is going to come up with an image, but it will usually end up being a fantasy image. This image is not going to be based on reality; it is going to be based on anything that the child can find that the parent does value, and it will include a lot of hidden weaknesses. This is going to grow over time, and while the child is going to start seeing this as reality, it is far from it and can cause some issues.

*Body image*

Studies have seen that there is a strong relationship between the body esteem of a woman and narcissism. American society still loves the idea of being beautiful, and one of the measures of this beauty is with thinness. However, evidence shows that now it is not just women who worry about their bodies, but also males. To be sure, there has been a huge rise in eating disorders that include both genders.

Distorted and excessive concerns with the body have been linked with not just eating disorders in many studies, but also with narcissism. Research on this has suggested that the personality characteristics that we find with bulimics will match up pretty closely with some of the traits that are found with NPD.

This one is a hard thing to find. Our lives are bombarded with images of those who have perfect bodies, and much of this is to sell us a service or product. Seeing these images are going to have a big influence on young adults and children. What is even worse is that it is not just in advertising and the media that is doing this. It is possible that some parents are going to be too overly critical about the way their children act, look or talk, which can harm the self-esteem of the child.

## Mirroring

Another thing to look at is the idea of mirroring. Mirroring is basically how a child feels admired or noticed. You might describe it as the gleam in the parents' eyes when they are looking over at their children. These children want to see the smiles and the approval when they look to their parents. Because of this, there are many theorists who believe that the understanding that children have of themselves come from two places including:

1. The right amount of approval and mirroring
2. The understanding of the values that the parents have.

This mirroring is going to help the child to develop a realistic sense of themselves. Without this mirroring, the child may find that they are stuck with needing to find and get approval from others in order to feel like they are fine. Or they may have a much-exaggerated need to feel admired and noticed by those around them. Without the understanding of the ideals from the parents, the child is going to stick with a very underdeveloped fantasy about themselves.

# Denial of feeling

You may find that another discussion that comes here is going to be about how important it is that a parent accepts the vulnerabilities of the child. And if there are any weak expressions that come out, or hurt feelings, they should not be reprimanded. Every child can and will have a time when they feel humiliated, rejected, or hurt. But it is important that the child doesn't start to fear these things happening. If the child does start to fear these normal emotions, they will just start to deny their feelings altogether. This allows them to not feel hurt and to stay strong, calm, and cool.

## Does neglect or pampering cause narcissism?

There are two schools of thought that come up here. Some researchers believe that it is neglect that is going to make narcissism come out. And then there are those who believe that pampering and over-indulging the child will cause this narcissism. But which of these theories is the right one?

In recent years, there are a lot of social learning theorists who believe that the development of NPD is the result of those parents who overvalue their children, the ones who are unrealistic, and the ones who pamper their children too much. These are the parents who make sure that their child has everything and anything that they could ever need, and they will do everything that they need to protect that child from any pains or hurt feelings.

While there is nothing wrong with loving your child and providing them, it is commonly agreed that your children need to be allowed to fail, to have some feelings of frustration, and to learn some positive ways to deal with the stumbling blocks that come up in life. Too much love can be spoiling, and this causes the children to feel that they are way more special than others. Too much love, if it is used improperly, can be a type of seduction. Some theories claim that too much love and spoiling may lead to the type of narcissistic behavior in which control and seduction of others are used to get needed admiration.

## Parents who are narcissists

If you have a narcissistic parent, you are more likely to have NPD as well. If anything, it is going to influence the development of the personality of the child. A parent who has NPD, often the father, may see that the child is a threat to their needed narcissistic supply. Though there are some times when the reverse is true and a parent could see this child as the source of narcissistic supply. Because of this, the parent would encourage the child to obey, adore, and idolize them. If the child ends up invading the space of the father though, they may try to limit this by humiliating, hurting, or belittling them.

Now, it is also possible that the mother will be the one who has NPD. When this happens, there is usually an issue where the child's and mother's roles are reversed. Instead of taking care of the needs of the child, the mother will make their child take care of their needs.

# How to minimize these behaviors

Regardless of how the NPD starts in an individual, it is important to learn how to minimize these behaviors as much as possible. Experts, no matter what side of things they are on, will agree that there are some measures that you could consider doing in parenting that can minimize the development of NPD and other behaviors that are considered narcissistic. Some of these will include:

1. Take the time to recognize and even acknowledge the real achievements of your child.
2. Encourage your child to explore the skills and talents that they are good at. But also take time to identify those that they can, or need, to work on.
3. Help your child to understand that for most people, the rewards that they get are the result of hard work and a lot of discipline, rather than it being easy as they see in the movies.
4. Try to encourage children to be more involved in the community and to help out those who need it.
5. Tell a child no, but try to do it in an empathetic way. This shows the child that there is nothing bad for requesting or asking for something, and they are still loved, even if you have to say no.
6. You need to learn how to set boundaries on a consistent basis and have limits, without criticizing the child when they act out a bit.
7. Think about how you are able to give your children their own voice. This doesn't mean that they get complete control over everything, but they still get a say.

8. Allow the child to feel loved, good, and not at fault for wrongdoing or for any failures in their efforts.

# Chapter 5: What Happens to the Person with NPD without Treatment?

While there are a number of treatments that the patient can choose to go with in order to get help and to leave some of those personality traits behind there are times when the narcissist is going to either never get help or will choose to not get help at all. This can lead to a number of issues along the way, depending on the person and how bad the narcissism is.

## Splitting as a defense

Without the proper treatment for the individual, in order to function on a daily basis, the person who is suffering from NPD will need to use a few defense mechanisms to help them out. While there is nothing wrong with these defenses (many people use them on a regular basis for their emotional health), they can cause some issues when the narcissist starts to rely on them.

The narcissist may start to rely on these in a normal way in order to deal with some of the hurtful emotions they have including anger, fear, grief, and anxiety. Remember that these defenses are there and they exist so that people can defend themselves against feelings that will overwhelm or threaten them, or with any other feelings that people are not prepared to deal with yet. Healthy defense mechanisms, when they are used in the proper manner, are going to be so helpful when it comes to maintaining self-esteem and a self-image that is positive.

All of us are going to have different defenses that are going to become ways of coping with any and all of the stresses that show up in our lives. There are often going to be two categories that these defense mechanisms will rely on including the primitive and the more advanced ones that can develop over time. Let's take a look at how each one of these works and why it is so important to start understanding each one.

## Primitive Defense Mechanisms

These kinds of mechanisms are going to show up in infancy. At this time, there is going to be a very limited grasp of reality, and there is going to be no real sense of self. This is a real big time when a person can start developing some problems, especially emotional problems, including narcissism.

These primitive defenses are the ones that you will start using as a very young child. It is often going to include withdrawal, where the child is going to start removing themselves emotionally from that moment. As the infant starts to withdraw, they are able to disconnect from the real world, and they are going to live for a time in a different place, one where they are away from their feelings, thoughts, and other memories that could be painful.

Then there could be the issue of denial. This is when the child is going to refuse to accept fact or reality. They may act like that painful feeling, thought, or event didn't even happen at all. Primitive idealization is the way in which a child is going to see their parents as being superhuman, the ones who are able to swoop in and protect the child from all the pain and the evils, the ones who are able to come in and fix everything.

Another one of these primitive defense mechanisms, the one that narcissists are the most likely to use, is known as splitting. This splitting is kind of like all-or-nothing thinking, where the person is going to see things in only black and white. When this splitting happens, people or things will either be all bad or all good. This is still something that comes from infancy. The

baby is going to see that when their needs are met and they are satisfied, or when they see their mother, that all is good. When they are frustrated, all is bad.

Of course, in this reality, the baby is not able to see reality, and they may not realize that they are seeing it in black and white. It is perfectly normal for a baby to act in this way because they don't understand the world that is around them. But, if this starts to follow the child into their adult life, it can end up with some problems.

In some ways, this splitting is going to be similar to a broad type of stereotyping, such as the statement "All the members of (insert group here) are lazy and dumb." Narcissists are not only going to use these statements on a regular basis to describe how all people are inferior to themselves, but they are going to use this splitting as a way to create the false image that they want.

People who have NPD are going to use splitting because it allows them to preserve the self-esteem that they have. When they see themselves as being entirely good, and they see everybody else as being entirely bad, they will find that it is easier to be superior to them. Splitting is often going to be right at the core of any instability in a relationship when a narcissist is involved. Because the narcissist is often going to see their spouse or the other person in the relationship, as either all good or all bad, it can cause a lot of unstable and violent mood swings in the process.

# How are others affected?

Now that we know a bit more about the narcissism and how it starts, it is important to take a quick look at how some of the loved ones of the person with the disorder are going to be affected as well. While it is common to have some ups and downs and some disagreements with those we love, narcissism is going to take this to the next level.

When we find out that a family member, or even a spouse, may have NPD, whether they are the parent or the sibling or a spouse or someone else, it is possible that those who are around them are going to be affected in a hurtful and a negative way.

For example, if the parent is the one with narcissism, it can cause some issues with them and their child. They will either decide that the child is competition to them getting the attention and love that they want, and so the child will be harmed, humiliated, and more to get them out of the way. Or the narcissist may decide that the child is the way that they are going to get the love and attention that they want, and they will groom them to provide that love and attention to them, rather than the child getting what they need.

It is so important for this narcissism to be taken care of as quickly as possible. The longer that this condition goes on, the harder it is going to be to fight it off and to get rid of the harmful effects that can come with it. Often, the narcissist is going to be reluctant to get the help that they need. But even if they don't, learning how to deal with the narcissism, and to get out of that situation, can help you to feel much healthier and better as well.

# Chapter 6: Treatments for NPD

Now that we know a bit more about NPD, what causes it, and how it can affect the individual and the ones who are around them, it is time to look at some of the different treatments that the person with NPD can work on to control the behaviors and to help them live a more normal life. There are a few different treatments that you can consider working with including:

## Individual therapy

When we look at individual therapy, the ultimate goal is to help these individuals unlearn some of the negative patterns of behavior and to learn better ways that they are able to relate to others. This allows them to have relationships that are rewarding, enjoyable, and more intimate.

These therapy sessions can be a nice place to start. They are designed to turn the mirror in a bit and to allow the person who is dealing with NPD to better understand the forces that drives them to be disrespectful, distrustful, and competitive to others. And then, with this light still shining on them, and with them having a level of discomfort about the whole thing, it helps them to find some of the best ways to cope with these inner demons so that they can live a better and more fulfilling life in the future.

When an individual with NPD decides to enter into individual therapy, there are going to be three stages that they will go through. They will move through these stages at their own pace, depending on how much work needs to be done, and how willing the individual is to doing this therapy. The three stages of individual therapy for NPD include:

1. The client and the therapist will get together and will go over some of

the specific feelings and thoughts in detail.

2. The client and the therapist are going to work together in order to identify which distorted views are there with the patient.
3. The therapist will then work with the client in order to entertain new ways of thinking, ones that are not distorted.

As the therapy progresses, it is likely that the therapist is going to give their client some specific homework assignments. These assignments can be unpleasant sometimes, it is going to help the person with NPD to identify verbal cues and keep track of the kinds of phrases and words that they use when they are talking about themselves and about others. The point of doing these is to help the client recognize the phrases that they use for themselves.

For example, one kind of assignment that may show up is that the therapist will ask the patient to pay attention to the I and me statements that they use for 24 hours. Or to keep track of how often they talk about themselves? Do they spend time interrupting the story that someone else is telling just to have their own tale heard? Many times, just being able to see how much the narcissist references back to their own experiences and their own lives in a day will be a big wakeup call for them.

When the client is in individual therapy for this disorder, the therapist is there to teach and to help with some recognition of the problem, without having any threatening presence there. The therapist is going to be subtle in their work so that the person with NPD will bend a bit and start to see new ways that they can behave and think. This is why it is so important to create a trusting and positive relationship between the client and the therapist.

# Psychotherapy

Another method for treating NPD is to use psychoanalytical therapy. This is a very Freudian method to use, but it isn't used as much with NPD as it once would. Basically, this model states that these emotional disorders are going to be based on some conflicts inside the person that are unresolved. These conflicts show up between the different aspects that come with someone's psyche, meaning their id, ego, and superego. To keep this simple, the conflict is going to come up between the unconscious and conscious mind.

The goal of doing individual psychodynamic therapy is to help reduce these conflicts. If the therapist can be successful, it means that the personality of the individual is going to change in the process as well.

With this kind of treatment, the therapist is likely to take a less active role. They are going to stay quiet for quite a bit of the process, and they may rely on the patient to reveal an increasing amount of distress that is buried down deep. Another thing that is used in this kind of therapy is the idea of dreams. Freud believed that the conflicts that come up in the subconscious brain are going to show up in dreams. Because of this, psychotherapy is going to take a look at dreams in order to try and gain some insights into their meaning and to see some more about the inner struggle of the patient.

# Group therapy

You will find that when you deal with a narcissist, you are dealing with an extreme individual. These individuals are going to walk around believing that they are not only the person in the whole world, but they may even believe that they are the only person in the room. Because of this, it shouldn't surprise us too much that these people are going to have difficulties when they end up in a group.

Because of this, the effectiveness of going with a group therapy setting is questionable. The narcissist is often going to upset the group dynamic that is being set up, both in work and other social situations, and they are not going to be very open to some collaborative efforts, which is what needs to happen for group therapy to be effective.

However, some agree that forcing the narcissist to work with a group going with an in-patient environment can be a little bit useful. The need to work in a team, to listen to the person in charge, and to learn how to respect the other people in the group may be enough to help break off the behaviors of narcissism that are found. However, it is important that some caution should be taken in order to make sure that the narcissist doesn't take over, or start to manipulate the group the way they want.

# Cognitive Behavioral Therapy

The basis of CBT is to help the person who is suffering from NPD to learn how to find the untrue beliefs and their negative behaviors, and then replace them with positive and healthy ones. The basis of this therapy is that our feelings, and the way that we think about things, is going to play a big role in how we are able to interact with others and the world that is around us.

The goal of this therapy is to get the patient to realize that while they are not able to control all the aspects of their lives and they can't control the world and how it acts around them, they do have some power over how they interpret and choose to deal with the events and the people they encounter on a regular basis. When it comes to those who are suffering from NPD, CBT has proven to be a really effective way to deal with the problem.

# Medications to control the symptoms

NPD can sometimes be treated with some medication as well. Often, the patient is first going to work with one or more of the long-term talk therapies that we described before. And there usually aren't any drugs or other medications that are specifically prescribed in order to treat the NPD itself.

Even with this, there are some medications that have been used throughout time to help the patient deal with the symptoms that come with NPD. Taking medications to help with anxiety, depression, and other emotional distress issues can sometimes be an option that the patient takes.

Of course, since there hasn't been a definitive biochemical basis for NPD as of yet, it is unlikely that any drugs to specifically treat the condition are going to be developed, at least for now. For the most part, therapies are still the most respected way to help with recovery. Sometimes, when the case is really severe, some anxiety and depression medications can be used to help, but they are used in addition to the talk therapies, not on their own.

When it comes to working with someone who is suffering from NPD, it is important for them to go through some kind of therapy. This will ensure that they are able to take care of the issues that are causing NPD, and can allow them to form relationships that are more meaningful and bring them more joy. The talk therapies that are presented in the chapter above are often recognized as the best options to help the patient deal with their narcissism.

# Chapter 7: Other Methods to Deal with NPD

In addition to some of the talk therapies that we looked at above, there are sometimes some other therapies that can be used to help with this condition as well. These are going to have varying degrees of success, based on how the narcissist sees themselves, and if they are willing to actually take the steps necessary to make changes. Some of the other methods that can be used to help deal with NPD include:

## Healing Strategies

Individuals who are dealing with NPD and narcissism have been very vocal online and in various forums that professionals lead. These individuals are able to share some of their own experiences and can offer a few healing strategies that will be useful to a lot of those who are dealing with this condition. Some of the suggestions that these individuals have offered up include:

1. Use goal setting skills in order to help you reach a goal that makes you feel good, rather than always trying to impress others.
2. Develop some interests and hobbies and then earn more about it to preoccupy your time.
3. Develop some social skills so that you are able to keep and make friends. Learn how to be interested in others, not to interrupt, and how to be empathetic. Make healthy friends who like each other, without any strings connected.
4. Learn how to love and relax. Learn that other people can be loved just for being normal, without them having to provide some benefit to you.
5. Find and identify any of the examples of you belittling someone else,

whether you do it out loud or in your head.

6. Find and identify situations where one feels entitled. List things that were done to impress.

7. Find and identify some of the faulty assumptions that you started to make early on in your life, the assumptions that you made that would be the basis for some of the behaviors that you have now.

## Lifestyle Changes

Another thing that you are able to work with here are some lifestyle changes. If either you or a loved one is looking into therapy for NPD, then you need to take some time to think about the questions that are the most important to ask. You can even rehearse them a bit or take some notes to ensure that you get them answered. Some of the things that you can consider doing to make small changes in your own lifestyle include:

1. Ask questions that the other person is able to actually answer rather than trying to create a drama, a trial, or something to prove, to take revenge on, or to win.

2. Think about some of the truths, even if they are painful, about your parents, or your family that you may want to deal with at some point, but you might not be ready to confront at this time.

3. Don't feel like you need to sound like you already know it all or that you need to work with a special language. It is fine to speak the way that you want and to be yourself.

4. Look at it not like there is a big problem with you, something that others are trying to solve. Rather, use it as a way to make some adjustments for a happier and healthier you.

## Using the Twelve Step Program

You may find that from a healing standpoint, a person with narcissism will be able to benefit from the twelve step program in their lives. This could be because NPD can often look like addiction in a number of ways, and the

only difference is that the addict, instead of turning to drugs or alcohol, is turning to want to be adored and idolized by others.

This is the same twelve-step program that has been used by Alcoholics Anonymous for many years now, and it has been adapted many times over and over again to be used for different addictions depending on the recovery program. You can easily use it to help deal with the narcissistic issues as well, including:

1. We admitted that we are powerless over narcissism, that our lives had become unmanageable.
2. We came to believe that it would take a power greater than ourselves in order to restore our sanity to use.
3. We made a decision to turn our will, as well as our lives, over to the care of God, as we understood Him (this allows for different beliefs of a Higher Power to come into play, and didn't just make this work for Christians).
4. We made a searching and fearless moral inventory of ourselves.
5. We took the time to admit to ourselves, to God, and to someone else the exact nature of the wrongs that we did.
6. We were entirely ready to have God remove all of the defects that are in our character.
7. We were humble, and in that process, we asked Him to remove all of the shortcomings that we have.
8. We made a list of all of those who were harmed during our

narcissistic tendencies, and we became willing to make amends to all those who could.

9. We made direct amends to those who could, when it was possible, except when to do so would injure them or others.

10.       We continued on with our personal inventory and when we were wrong about something, we were quick to admit it.

11.       We sought, with the help of meditation and prayer, to improve our conscious contact with God, as we understand Him, praying only to have the knowledge of His will for us, and the power to carry it out.

12.       Having a spiritual awakening as the result of these twelve steps, we tried to carry this message and practice these in all of our affairs.

The thing to remember here is that for any of these methods to work, the narcissist must be open and willing to try them out. There are many times when the narcissist will have not want to make them work, and they will continually think that others have the problem, not them and that this whole thing is a waste of time.

If the sufferer isn't willing to make the changes, then it is unlikely that the narcissist is going to get better. Even if they have been dealing with this problem for some time, they will rebel against it and are not likely to agree to continue on with this journey. This can be difficult for the victim, or someone else close to the narcissist to deal with, but it is important, once the narcissist decides not to take treatment, to walk away and help keep yourself and your health going strong instead.

# Chapter 8: Exploring Some of the Lifestyles and Myths of NPD

As most people enter the world of being an adult, they are going to find reality, accept the person they are, and deal with the ups and downs that come in life by being the best that they can. But then there are some of those who find that it is hard to live a lifestyle that is normal. They want to keep being that superhero they were as a child, and they are not able to understand why things need to change. In this chapter, we are going to take a look at some of the myths and lifestyles of someone who has narcissism and why it is so important to understand what is real and what isn't.

## Is a little bit of narcissism healthy?

The way that we use the word narcissism in our modern world means that the answer to whether narcissism is healthy or not can go either way. It has its good side and its bad side. A healthy amount of narcissism is often seen as a good thing, like having an attitude that is confident. It's in people who know themselves, who are able to accept both their weaknesses and their strengths, and who have a sense of what is good and bad about them.

When there is a healthy amount of narcissism in the individual, it is going to include a level of self-love that makes the person want to look and do their best, while still balancing some appreciation, care, and love for others. Everyone is going to have a few traits that are narcissistic. It is part of both your early development as a child and your adult life. This is because we all have wants and needs, and there are going to be times when these show up more than others.

If you have a healthy amount of narcissism, and you use it to better yourself while still showing some compassion to those around you, then yes, a bit of narcissism is healthy in your life. It allows you to not get stepped on and put down by others all the time. And it makes it easier to know your own worth no matter who you are around.

## Loving without self-love

Love is a very interesting topic and one that a lot of people do not fully understand for themselves yet. Whether we are talking about love for others or self-love, it is something that people throughout the years are going to try their hardest to explain, even though they may come up short.

However, it is important to remember here that when it comes to self-love, you shouldn't confuse loving yourself (which all of us need to do on occasion), with unhealthy narcissism. In fact, many therapists have worked with those who have narcissism and NPD as those who don't have a lot of self-love. This is because when they take a look at themselves in the mirror, all they see is an image, rather than something that is true. Self-love is going to be loving yourself the way you are now and not the way you imagine yourself in your head. Self-love is going to be healthy, rather than selfish, and that is what distinguishes it from narcissistic tendencies.

In the Zen ideology, the idea of loving oneself is going to be all about the total dedication towards becomes a better person, about not needing to always be the top priority in each group, and about making sure that your emotional, mental, and physical health are all in line. With these ideas, a person is going to need to be available to put the needs of others first, to empathize with others, and to care about others.

While this does allow some room for you to stop and take care of yourself on occasion, it also recognizes that you need to be open and willing to take care of those around you as well. There are some theorists who will propose how self-love is going to be a more peaceful state of mind, one where

challenges are not able to bother you because you have earned how to be safe and balanced. This can do wonders when it comes to your inner strengths, and it will allow your abilities to shine out.

It is important for you to love yourself because once you are able to do that, it is possible to love others. There are many schools of thought that will talk about how important it is to be connected with those around you and to work on serving these individuals. And doing this is going to be hard if you don't have self-love for yourself. This is where a lot of narcissists are going to run into trouble. They don't realize that the image they love about themselves is a false one, and so they have no self-love. Since they don't love themselves, it is almost impossible for them to love or care about, or even help, those around them.

# NPD and How It Shows Up In the Workplace

This brings up an interesting point about how well the narcissist is able to perform in the workplace. They don't get along with others, and they constantly need to be the center of attention in order to feel good. This can seem to make it difficult for them to get along with others and do well at work. But everywhere we look, even at work, there are going to be narcissist around as well.

There has been some recent research that shows that narcissists have what it takes to be leaders. This is because, even though they may use people and not get along with others, they have a lot of leadership characteristics like competitiveness, assertiveness, energy, and motivation. However, just because they have these characteristics doesn't mean that they are going to be successful, and it is possible that, whether or not they become successful, they could cause some problems for those who work there, and for the business as a whole.

One issue that comes up here is that the narcissist is not going to like a compromise, admitting that they are the one who did the error or failure. And all of these things are going to be natural parts of doing business and of working. Not accepting them can cause some issues about this.

While there are a lot of narcissists in the world around us, it is important to know that there is a downside. Yes, they can bring some great traits to leadership and they can be really good at their job if they are interested in doing it well, but often, these people are going to be the ones who cause problems in the business, and it is even worse because the narcissist doesn't see that they are the one who caused the damage. They may choose to distort the issue or deny that they had anything to do with it. These narcissists are going to work to justify themselves or they will make a lot of rationalizations that will help to make their own self-worth go up but won't do any good for anyone else.

This is why many companies need to be careful about who they are working with. There are some narcissists who are able to rein it in a bit and can keep doing an amazing job as managers. But if the narcissist is not able to control themselves, and they run into trouble accepting things, or admitting that they are wrong, it is possible that the narcissistic leader will end up taking the company and leading it to the ground.

Remember that these narcissists are not going to be that fond of learning from others. They like to be the ones who dominate, the ones who make speeches, and they are not likely to listen to others. Even though they like to be surrounded by a big group of women and men who agree with everything they say, the narcissist has no true want to do teamwork.

Working with a boss who is a narcissist is going to be difficult. They are going to be demanding, will not listen to your requests or concerns at all, no matter how valid these are, and they can make your workspace really hard to deal with. Some of the tips that you can keep in mind in order to avoid some of the potential problems with a narcissistic boss include:

1. Try to keep some good records of the work that you do. This helps you in case any narcissistic managers or coworkers start to

misinterpret your intentions. It also keeps them from taking credit for the accomplishments and work that you are doing.

2. Keep all of the communication you do with them professional. It is sometimes tempting to confide in the narcissist, but if you do that, be prepared for them to take your words and use them to their own advantage if they need.

3. It can be hard to deal with this kind of boss. But remember that the issues have nothing to do with you, and are more about the narcissism.

4. If you feel that your boss is making a decision that is really bad, you can still give your opinion. But the best way to do this is to show them your alternative and then discuss how the narcissist is personally going to be able to benefit from this change.

5. Make sure that they know your personal boundaries and that you expect them to stick with these.

# Narcissism and Workaholics

Since it is now more common than ever to find narcissism in the workplace, it seems more likely that there is a link between the narcissistic personality traits and those who are typically called workaholics. Hard work is a good thing, just like having self-confidence can be a good thing. But when either of these is blown out of proportion too much, it is going to end up harming others. And when work is carried to the point where it excludes all else, it is going to be workaholism and it can be harmful to the narcissist and everyone who is related or near the.

There is no denying that the people of America are hardworking people. And it seems that in our current economy and with wages staying pretty stagnant, people are working more now than ever. It isn't uncommon to find people working two or three jobs in the hopes of making ends meet. But there is a difference between working hard to get by or because you love your job and the issues of workaholism.

When we are looking at the workaholic, it seems like everything and anything is going to come behind the work, even family. Vacation and social engagements are not going to be a part of their life. And they will basically become their job, not allowing anything else to come in. And often, this is going to come with narcissism because the workaholic is able to define their sense of self with the job. To the workaholic, the job is going to be a false image of who they are, and it is so important to them because it allows them to escape from reality, just like the false sense of the narcissist does.

With so many similarities that are showing up between the personalities of a workaholic and a narcissist, it is no wonder that *Psychology Today* recently published a study that found that those who are admitted workaholics are going to score highly on a personality scale that measures obsessive perfectionism and narcissism.

Want to see how close these two personality traits are to each other? We have already gone through and talked about some of the personality traits that come with being a narcissist, now let's explore some of the traits that you are going to see with a workaholic. When we are looking at a workaholic, we are looking at a person who:

1. Pursues power and values self-importance to help support a grandiose image of their self-worth and to get more admiration from those they work with.
2. Overproduce in order to make themselves be above, or at least seem superior, to those they work with.
3. They let work become almost an obsession, in a similar manner that a narcissist works to fill their narcissistic supply. These people are only able to find the value in themselves through their work.
4. These people are going to see some expectations of themselves that are unrealistic. They expect that their performance needs to be perfect.
5. They are very impatient about getting to the next level.
6. They are compulsive.
7. They are really into using busyness as a defense to escape from some of the emotional commitments that they have or some of the negative emotions that they need to work with.

When we get down to the roots of both problems, we see that workaholism and narcissism are both going to be conditions that result from either a poorly defined sense of self or one that is false. Being able to develop this healthy sense of self is going to require a feeling of identity and of being worthwhile, and it needs to develop separately from either the failures or the accomplishments of the individual. But while this may be something that most people are able to work with, it is something that both workaholics and narcissists struggle with.

As you can see, working with a narcissist and understanding how this whole process works is something that is going to take some time and effort in order to accomplish. These people can often take over as a leader, and since they don't have empathy for others, it is sometimes difficult to work with them. Knowing how to look out for this personality type and working to protect yourself can make working in that situation easier over time.

# Chapter 9: How to Ask for Help When Dealing with a Narcissist

When you are on the receiving end of narcissism, it is hard to figure out what to do. You need to know that it is perfectly fine and okay for you to take a step back from this relationship, no matter who they are and take care of yourself. You need to know what to do and how to do something for yourself so that you can start to feel good as well.

Of course, asking for help can sometimes be difficult to do in these situations. Often when you need this help with a narcissist, it is because you have been with them for a long time, or you are in what you thought was an intimate relationship with them. This can make you feel like you did something wrong like you are too weak, or like others are going to make fun of you. But it is nearly impossible to be with a narcissist and to handle it on your own without some help.

Asking for help is not a sign of weakness. It is a sign that you are ready to start taking care of yourself and you are ready to stop putting the narcissist first. When you are ready to start reaching out for help, who are you going to reach out to? And what kind of help is there for you when you want to deal with this narcissist? Let's take a look at some of the options that are available to you, and what you can do when you are ready to change the relationship and you need help dealing with a narcissist.

# When should I ask for help?

As soon as you notice that you are dealing with a narcissist, it is time to get the help that you need. Don't feel bad if you have been in the relationship for some time. Narcissists know that if they come on too strong in the beginning, they will scare others away from them. If no one will be around the narcissist, then the narcissist will not be able to get their fill of attention and love from that chosen person.

Because of this, the narcissist is often going to be able to trick you into not realizing what is going on. They will seem like they are loving, that they are a sweet talker, and like they are the one for you. By the time most people figure out that they are dealing with this narcissist, they have been together or in some kind of relationship for a long time.

Don't let this stop you from getting the help that you need. Yes, it may seem like you are making things up. And maybe you worry that feeling this way means that you were dumb and missed out on the signs. In reality, you probably did miss out on some signs, but the narcissist is really good at hiding themselves and making sure that you can't see these signs until it is too late.

So, it is best if you are able to take a stand and ask for help as soon as you realize that you are dealing with a narcissist. Even if it is hard. Even if it feels like you are going to look like a fool and that others are going to make fun of you. Even if you worry that you are seeing things or making things up in your head. If you start to suspect that you are dealing with a narcissist, then it is likely that you truly are, and you need to get the help that you can as early as possible.

## Taking those first steps

There are a lot of men and women who will go through the same experience of dealing with narcissism. Maybe they knew a child, a friend, a parent, a sibling, a lover, a spouse or someone else who seemed to have the real problem with narcissism. It is something that all of us have heard about. It seems that with our current culture and the media that is around us, it is easier than ever to hear about and meet up with narcissists of all kind.

Because of the media and other things that go on around us, we may wonder if we are actually dealing with someone who is a narcissist, or if we are just blowing the picture up too big in our heads. One good way to check is to see how the person responds when you try to talk through it with them. Maybe if you go and talk about how it feels like you haven't been able to see your friends in some time. If they agree and then suggest you should set up a girl's night out or something similar, then it's likely that life has just gotten in the way, and that is why you haven't had time to go out with friends.

But, when you are dealing with a narcissist, they don't want you to have any connections, outside of the connection that you have with them. They want you to just take care of them, so suggesting that you go out with some friends and family would be a foreign idea to them. They may get defensive about it, try to tell you that it is a bad idea, and will try to do everything in their power to not let you go, while still making it look like it was your idea.

If you are pretty sure that you are dealing with someone who is a narcissist, then it is time to get some help. Of course, it is not always hard to think about getting help to feel okay, but this is a good thing to do. Many of those who figure out that they are in a relationship with someone who is a narcissist may feel ashamed to ask anyone else for help and they may think, wrongly of course, that they were not smart enough or have enough resilience in order to do the work themselves.

The first step is to realize that you are dealing with someone who is a narcissist. Since the narcissist is often going to do what is in their power to ensure you don't realize this fact because this means that they lose out on their supply, just getting with this breakthrough is going to make a big difference in your own overall health and well-being. Once you realize this, you will be able to take the next step in looking for the right help, both for you and for the person who suffers from narcissism.

# A case study of the demoralized woman

Let's look at an example of what can happen in a narcissistic relationship. One young woman, who is typical of many others regardless of their gender, had written online about how she had to ask for help in order to help herself and others who may have been in a similar situation as her. After being in a relationship for five years with a man she had thought was her dream man, she found that her world ended up collapsing around her. She found that it was hard to cope.

It had actually been an escalating nightmare for those five years. She talked about how she felt so alone and lost in that relationship, not really understanding how things happened, or why they ended up happening. Because of the boyfriend's constant demoralizing and berating, she believed that all the things wrong and all of the things that didn't go right in that relationship were her fault. Yet, even with this going on, she still wanted to keep this man in her life, though he had gone on and found another girlfriend.

Over time, while she was dealing with this and still trying to figure out how to get the man she loved back, she revealed some of the situations to one of her friends. At the time, the friend suggested that she go and see her own therapist. After doing an evaluation, the therapist told this woman that her boyfriend was a narcissist. The woman had to then figure out how to accept this truth. This man, who was most likely a narcissist, could not feel compassion, empathy, or love for her.

With some therapy and some time, this woman reached a point where she was able to realize that this man, no matter how much she had loved him, had been able to deplete all of your mental, emotional, and physical energy, and then he was able to leave when there was no more left to give. This is when she realized that it was time to ask for help.

## Whom should you ask for help?

The story above is similar to what a lot of women, and sometimes even men, will experience when they get in a relationship with a narcissist. They are led to believe that they are worthless and that all of the problems that come up in the relationship are their own fault. They are told that they are worthless and that they are not perfect. And yet, they cling to that person, loving them through it all. Once the narcissist is able to take everything they can from the victim, they leave, without feeling any remorse or anything else.

Going through this situation can leave you feeling a bit embarrassed, and you may find it hard to talk to those around you. But, if you do have a potential narcissist or a narcissist in your life, then all health professionals agree that you need to have at least two people on your side as support. These include a family member and a trustworthy friend who will listen to your feelings, listen to your fears, and help with the pain. You should also consider working with a professional who will be able to answer any of the questions that you have at this time, and who will be able to give you an objective way to deal with the situation.

If you are not able to find a close friend or family member to work with, don't let this stop you from getting the help that you need. If you have been dealing with a narcissist, you are probably feeling lost and alone. And if you have been in a relationship with one for a longer period of time, then you may have alienated a lot of your friends and family and have no one to turn to. Don't let this keep you back from getting the help that you need.

Finding a professional to help you, even if you are not able to get the narcissist to get treatment too, will do a ton of good. They will be able to discuss if your partner really was a narcissist, what all of this means, and can help you to handle the situation in a way that will guide you to your own self-esteem and self-worth coming back. This can help you deal and get your life back on track after all of the things that the narcissist was able to take from you.

# How to deal with the varied reactions

Of course, we all know those people who are quick to judge others, and usually, they are willing to do this in a negative, rather than a positive, manner. And that can happen when you decide to become open about the narcissist in your life. Even when you do it to some of the people you are closest to in your life, they may not understand the situation or the decisions that you make for yourself and your children as this situation gets worse. This is even harder to do if the narcissist had met some of these people and made a great outward appearance to them.

Depending on your own family, telling them about being with a potential narcissist will not get you the response that you are looking for. They may say things like "All men are dogs" "Just give him time" or even "You have to be joking, no way, he's so charming and special". This can happen with your friends as well. And many times, this happens because the narcissist has done such a good job of deceiving those around them.

This can be hard to deal with. You want to get some help and support, but others are just not seeing the damn thing that you are. They assume that you are seeing it the wrong way, or that you are just lying to get them to go against the narcissist. And when others are unfair to you or choose not to listen to what you are saying, it can make the situation even harder to deal with

## How can I help someone with NPD?

Caring about and wanting to help the narcissist means that you are already coming to this situation with goodness and concern. As for the narcissist, what can be done for them is always at the forefront of their lives. So, one important thing that you can do here is to take a step back, find out how you can detach, and then use the empathy that you have in life in order to understand and try to be helpful.

While there are many therapists who believe that a narcissist is able to change for the better, it is something that takes a lot of work. It is possible for you to get the whole thing off to a good start, but it is usually going to be some sort of mental health professional who will be able to help the narcissist. Seeing a therapist for yourself can make it easier to handle the problems as well. Depending on the situation and how willing the narcissist is to doing the work, you may see a therapist on your own, the therapist may work with you and the narcissist separately, or you and the narcissist may do some therapy together.

Some of the best things that you can do to help you get started with getting them the help that they need, and to ensure that you really know what is going on here, include:

1. Ask your partner, the one with NPD, to write down what they expect from you, and any of the places where they think you are falling short. Consider any of the points that are reasonable and then ignore the rest. Inform your partner about what you think is on the list that is

   unreasonable and explain why. Let them know that this is not up for argument or discussion.

2. To help the person with NPD to choose to go to some kind of counseling, whether it is marriage or single counseling, you can tell them that you need them to help bring the relationship back to the intimacy, love, and warmth that it used to have.

3. Admit that there are some faults of your own that you would like to get fixed so that you can be a better spouse. This helps them to see that counseling is not just all about them, so they are more willing to go. Of course, this is not a place where the narcissist is allowed to take that admission and rattle off a long list of your shortcomings. Be firm in this. If the narcissist starts doing that, then tell them the conversation is over and walk away.

4. You can sometimes appeal to the narcissism that is there by humoring your partner until you are able to get some better advice from a professional so you know the best way to proceed.

Another thing to consider here is that you probably shouldn't go home and then proclaim that your pattern is a narcissist. This is going to put anyone on the defensive, whether they are a narcissist or not, and can cause a lot more problems than it is going to solve. Instead, you can try to make some changes in your lifestyle. For example, if they try to interrupt you when you are talking, stop and say something like "I was finishing my story. Please let me continue. It hurts my feelings when you interrupt because it makes me feel like you don't value what I have to say." This works nicely because it lets you call out the behavior that is bothering you, gives a small goal for the narcissist to focus on and makes sure that you are able to concentrate on your feelings as well.

# How to help yourself

Along with this idea is the fact that you need to take care of yourself. You have spent some time working on making the narcissist happy, making sure that their needs are met. And it is likely that you have gone for some time without having any of your needs met or your feelings listened to in some time. During this time, it is important that you stop and learn how you can take care of yourself as well. Some of the things that you can do if you find that this relationship has done a number on your self-esteem include:

1. Spend time with those who think highly of you.
2. Do some activities that you find enjoyable, ones that make you feel great.
3. Do something that is good for yourself.
4. Join up for some kind of community or service group. You can even consider signing up for school or just a few classes.
5. Develop some new hobbies and take the time to actually do them.
6. Work on expanding out your circle of friends. You want to make sure that these are friends that are separate from the narcissist, ones that are healthy and good for you.
7. Try to make up your own support group, one that has at least three healthy adults. This helps you to get some new points of view and will make sure that you learn the differences between healthy behaviors and unhealthy ones.

If you can get the narcissist to agree to help, then this is great news. But in many cases, you are going to be the one who will go for help, and this is fine, too. You have been through a big experience, and taking the time to come out of that and to realize your own self-worth is going to be just as important as anything else.

# Chapter 10: Understanding Megalomania

The next topic that we are going to take a look at is known as megalomania. Sometimes, you may find that living with someone who has NPD is going to be like living with a maniac. And this does make a bit of sense because narcissism used to go by a different name, megalomania. This term basically means power mad.

Not everyone who is a narcissist or who has NPD is going to be dealing with the megalomania. This term is usually reserved for those who are in one of the most destructive and most extreme forms of NPD. The megalomaniac is going to have a need for absolute control and total power of those they are around. This means that when they are around another person, they are going to want to be in control over how that victim talks, walks, dresses, and thinks.

If you are reading through this, and you are worried that this is the exact situation that you yourself are dealing with, know that you are not alone in this. In fact, narcissism is often one of the few pathological conditions that are going to cause more pain and duress not to its sufferers, but to those who are closest to the one with NPD.

# The role that low self-esteem has to play

When you hear about the word megalomania, it is likely to bring up an image of someone who is pretentious, egotistical, and conceited, and other signals that are going to be useful when you want to describe a narcissist. But under all of this self-importance and arrogance is going to be like a self-esteem that is very fragile and may not even exist all that much. That is why, even with all of the noise and the bravado, those who are dealing with narcissism are going to struggle when it comes to even minor amounts of criticism.

When working with megalomania, despite what we may assume, you may find someone who, on the inside, is easily going to feel humiliated or ashamed. And when they feel this way on the inside, they are going to try and make themselves feel better, usually by going into a rage. They may decide that there is a need for them to belittle others in order to make up for the things that are missing or lacking in themselves.

Many psychologists are going to agree that while most narcissists are going to believe in that false image that they show the world, they do not feel that what makes up this image is going to be enough for them to really be better or superior to those around them. If they did, they would not need to constantly be around others, or constantly be looking for praise, in order to feel better.

There are times when a person who is suffering from NPD will show their true selves and they may reveal this low self-image to some. But when this happens, they are going to do it in a way to get compliments to feed their egos and to help them feel better. In one online forum, a husband is going to talk about this situation with a wife who had NPD. In this situation, he talked about how his wife would say negative things about herself and be self-deprecating. But over time, he started to see that it was all an act. All that this wife wanted was for her husband to constantly tell her how wonderful she was. Then, when he started to realize what was going on, he stopped giving the compliments.

Whether a narcissist is going to have low self-esteem or high self-esteem has been very controversial over the years. There are a lot of researchers believe that the push for high self-esteem, which a lot of self-help gurus and motivational speakers are going to push hard, and the praise that is heaped on a lot of young people to encourage them, could be a major reason that the cases of narcissism have risen. Whether it is because of this or because of low self-esteem that more narcissists tend to be showing up throughout the world is something that will need to be studied more in depth.

# Shame issues and NPD

Some researchers think that this narcissism is going to be a kind of defense that the individual can put up in order to protect themselves against shame. The narcissist may use shame in order to take that image they have made of their true self and protect them. It is a defense that is going to cause them a fight-or-flight response in those who are suffering from NPD, meaning that the individual will either run away or they will lash out.

Guilt can often cause a more personal response, such as asking the other person to forgive them or coming clean about the thing that they did wrong. But when it comes to shaming, this is going to come much more easily to the narcissist than that of guilt. It is possible for the narcissist to feel ashamed about the actions that they did, but will usually not admit that they have done something wrong.

Shame is going to be an emotional response to being imperfect or flawed. Many believe that it is tied into underlying low self-esteem, something that is found in some of the other problems that are tied to narcissism as well. While shame will have more to do with how the person feels about themselves, it can also be tied to what others think and how they are going to judge you. If a person believes that others see them as inferior, making a lot of mistakes, or lacking, it can lead to them feeling some shame

When we are talking about narcissism, this is going to be known as the grandiosity gap. This is going to be the difference between the information that the person with NPD gets from the real world and their false self-image. The greater the contrast between these two, the greater the gap and the greater the feelings of shame.

Many times, the narcissist wants to feel like they are separated from others by either being better than them or above them. But then they reach a conflict because they are seen as different from others and they have a fear of this. This is more of a feeling of otherness that they have to deal with. Narcissists are going to feel ashamed of their flaws, and any imperfections that make them different from other people. And this can cause even more problems than before.

## Covering for weaknesses vs. real strength

Outwardly, the narcissists, especially if they are described by therapists as megalomaniacs, are going to appear to the outside world as confident, powerful, and strong. But when you really dig down deep and learn more about them, you will find that the opposite is true. What appears to be strength on the outside is simply, in the case of a megalomaniac, covering up for some of the weaknesses that are on the inside.

In fact, one way to distinguish healthy narcissism from unhealthy narcissism is the fact that the former is going to recognize their own strengths while still accepting the weaknesses. But someone with NPD is not going to even have the ability to look and see that they are made up of traits that are both bad and good. They see anything that may be a bit negative about themselves as a weakness, and so, they will try to hide it, and overcompensate so that this negative won't show up in their image.

Many narcissists, but specifically those who are megalomaniacs, are going to see that the world is in absolutes, with no area for greys in there. They, and everything else that is found in their world will either be all good or all bad, and there is no in between with this. When we take a look into their minds, we see that they want to be all powerful, and this is impossible if they have any weaknesses at all.

Unlike the typical narcissist, people who accept that they can have strength, along with some weaknesses, understand that they don't need to be the best or the most powerful at everything in order to be successful. This is how normal people are going to view the world. It doesn't mean that we really

like the weaknesses that we have, but that we are willing to accept them. With a narcissist, they turn this around and just overcompensate or say that they don't have any weaknesses at all.

# Kohut's Model

One of the leading theorists of narcissism that we need to take a look at here is going to be Heinz Kohut. His work is the basic foundation of treating and understanding narcissism.

All humans are going to share the experience as children where they have a grandiose self-image and they idealize parents as the caregivers who are willing to give in and cater to all the needs of the child. With this in mind, Kohut was the first to suggest that narcissism could be a stunted form of development as we enter into adulthood.

In his writing, Kohut explains that as most children develop, they start to see more of the reality of the world, and their grand illusions are going to be replaced so that they can mature. When someone goes through a healthy development, the illusions of grandiosity that they had in the past are going to slowly move over as they gain more self-esteem. But if something happens, often some kind of emotional trauma, this primitive image of the self is going to stay intact and it won't change. And this is what happens in narcissistic personality disorder.

To look a bit more at his work, Kohut would describe a person with NPD as quick to anger, edgy, and irritable. The rage that would often show up in a narcissist would be the result of narcissistic wounds that occurred to that false image we talked about before. Kohut went on to say that the key to overcoming this disorder was to teach this person what empathy is all about. This is the main goal of all good therapies for treating NPD. Once the narcissist is able to empathize with others, they are going to be able to handle dealing with their self-esteem and fixing some of the other issues that may come up.

# Cultural considerations

While this disorder is not just found in the United States, many people think that the foundations as well as the modern values of modern America are more likely to promote this narcissism. The main stressors that are common in our modern society are going to include things like isolation, loneliness, and alienation. And then, to make the matter worse, our culture is going to teach us that it is best to withdraw when we are confronted with a situation that is stressful. Because of this, it is no surprise that narcissism is so common in the United States, and with other countries who value individualism.

It is possible that people in other countries are going to develop this disorder as well. But the modern society in America and the things that a lot of the people in this society value can make narcissism turn into an epidemic. There are a lot of reasons for this. It could be because people value being isolated and alone. And it could be because many parents are being overindulgent, providing a huge reward on accomplishments, even if they are minor. This may seem like good parenting, but it can make children feel like they are super special and that they should always get recognition for their accomplishments, no matter how big or small.

Another thing that could be causing the rise in narcissism is that there is no longer the value in our culture, as there was in the past, that pridefulness is a sin. There are pastors out there now who will preach that God wants us to be rich. There are sports celebrities who say that selfishness is actually a virtue. There is this pride in everything, and it is causing some issues all around.

To add to this is the fact that many people find that they work and live as separate individuals, apart from others and even freelancing because of the use of technology. There are a ton of advantages to being able to telecommute, such as more job opportunities, spending more time with your family, and more, but if you spend all day only interacting with a piece of technology could mean that we start to lose some of our humanity.

Since working alone means that you do not need to rely on others as much, and you don't need to show consideration to keep the peace at work, and you don't need to make compromises, it is easier to fall into some of the tendencies of narcissism.

It is important to note that people who have NPD can be driven by shame and fears. They are fearful of being made fun of, of others abandoning them, and to appear that they are lacking or that they have weaknesses of any kind. The increased amount of isolation socially in our digital era is going to increase this issue and can mean that more and more people are going to deal with narcissism over time. It can also end up taking them out of an environment in which they may see that their negative behavior is actually impacting others.

While living in this kind of world doesn't mean that you are automatically going to become a narcissist, it can increase the risk, and it means that more and more people are dealing with this issue. As there is a rise in narcissistic behavior of a world where the people only care about their own wants or needs without having any care of empathy of what others are going through, it may be time to make some changes before it gets out of hand.

# Chapter 11: Narcissism and Depression

After spending some time reading through this guidebook and learning more about narcissism, it can be really hard for you to feel any sorrow for them. And if you have been on the other side of this illness and seen how it can affect you, you are less likely to have any worries about their feelings. Narcissists are often going to come across to others as boastful, proud, and full of themselves. And because of this, it is really hard to see that there is a lot of self-confidence, self-esteem, and even depression issues underneath.

However, many of those who are narcissists are going to deal with a variety of other issues including depression. We are going to spend some time in this chapter taking a look at the link between narcissism and depression and how this is going to affect the sufferer.

# The depressive narcissists

When a narcissist enters into treatment, it is rare that they think that they are dealing with the narcissism. It is usually some other side effect, such as anxiety or depression, that will get them to go and seek help from a counselor. Of course, as we have described in this guidebook, there are a number of side effects that are going to come with narcissism, such as depression, eating disorders, and addition, and it is likely that the narcissist is going to enter into treatment because of one of these.

While those who have NPD often will not show a lot of the typical signs that come with mental illness, it is common for them to notice they are suffering some of the symptoms of depression, and they will seek help for this. Depression here is going to be linked to a term that is known as narcissistic wounds.

Many times, narcissists are going to feel depressed when they feel that they are losing or failure. They are going to come to a therapist or other counselor complaining that they feel empty, or that they are going to be bored easily when they aren't able to stimulate themselves on a higher level. Depression that shows up in a narcissist is going to be the result of repeated failures, whether these actually happened or they were imagined by the narcissist.

Usually, when you encounter a depressive narcissist, you will find that they are going to be big perfectionists. When life ends up not going like bland, which is what will happen at some point, depressive narcissists are more likely to blame themselves, and they can sometimes be overtaken with shame, something that leads them into even more depression than before.

If life with a narcissist is tough, then living with a depressed narcissist is going to seem like it is possible. Once they reach this state of depression, they may decide that it is time to turn everyone and everything around them into something that is negative. Their sense of melancholy can get so strong that everything the narcissist experiences can make them go into a deeper depression. This is a big swing, going from one side (being happy and joyful) to the other side (being down and depressed about everything).

When a narcissist starts to get depressed, it is possible that they may cry randomly, where before they would refuse to show emotions of any kind. Don't let this fool you though. Often, these tears are going to be crocodile tears so that they are able to get some sympathy and attention to substitute for that supply they are losing when it comes to attention.

It is during this stage where some other self-destructive behaviors like suicide attempts and self-mutilation could start showing up. But many times, these are going to be half-hearted. The narcissist doesn't really want to harm themselves or even kill themselves. Instead, they want to get attention to the action. If they are able to gain some sympathy and some attention out of the situation, then they see themselves as successful.

The biggest problem that can come up here is that for the most time, nothing that you try to do or say is going to snap the depressive narcissist out of their depression. This just turns into an additional defense mechanism that the narcissist is going to start relying on. This is a new persona that the narcissist is going to start relying on and anything that you try to do or say is going to be turned around, ensuring that it fits the worldview that the depressed narcissist has.

# Dealing with needs that are not met

Most of us realize that we are not always able to get what we want. But a true narcissist is going to have a lot of trouble dealing with this kind of advice, and they often won't decide to take that advice.

Despite what they think, those who have NPD are not always going to get what they want. This is often because they have expectations that are so high that they will never be able to get the thing that they need. And when they aren't able to get what they want; you end up with a narcissist who is going to cause a lot of trouble. If you are around this person, there are going to be violent temper tantrums and angry outbursts. And the narcissist is going to find that they end up with some form of depression as well.

Many of those who are around a narcissist feel like they are near a volcano that is about to explode. And often, the depression that comes out of this is going to be a reaction to these pockets of aggression that is buried down deep, but they refuse to acknowledge that there is anything going on. Depression in a narcissist is going to be a bit different than what you will see with others because it is more of aggression bottled up and then turned inward.

# Depression as the opposite of adoration

The main goal of most narcissists is to be adored and to have others idolize them. And if the narcissist could get others to worship them, then they would be even happier. But what would happen if this is not the case? You may think about the image of an aging screen star or a movie star who lost their beauty, their fame and fans, and then they retreat into themselves, crying over the past. This could be a good way to describe what the NPD person is going to feel when they stop getting some of the adoration that they need.

It is in the nature of humans to admire people, and it is common that you are going to put another person on a pedestal. They may do this with a celebrity, a coworker, relative, or a friend. What happens with this though is that the person who is placed on the pedestal may not have the abilities to hold up to the expectations that you have of this. And then, when you end up seeing that person for who they really are, they may not seem like they are as admirable as you had thought.

But this is going to turn into a horrible problem that you are going to need to deal with when the person you put on the pedestal happens to be a narcissist, and you live with them. When you met the narcissist in the beginning, it may be easy to place them on the pedestal. Many narcissists know how to be sexy, successful, charismatic, charming, and more in order to get you to pay attention and put your focus on them. This allows them to get put right on the pedestal where they want to be.

But, over time, and the more time you spend with them, you will find that the truth will start to come out, and you see that the narcissist doesn't really belong on that pedestal. When you decide to take them down, you are going to end up with some devastating effects, not only on the narcissist but also with yourself.

In any relationship, you may think that you have found the perfect partner to work with. And when you are in the beginning, it is likely that you are going to create an ideal version of the partner. You may know that there are some bad things, but you choose to just focus on the good. This happens in the early stages of any relationship, whether you are getting into it with a narcissist or with someone else. And this is exactly what the narcissist is hoping for when they start getting together with you.

As soon as you start to notice that your partner has flaws, which is going to come out at some point, it is going to improve a regular relationship. You start to know who the person really is, and you decide if you really love them for who they are. But for narcissists, when you find out their weaknesses and their flaws, it is like ripping their clothes off in public and then having them stand there wearing underwear for the whole world to see. As a result, the narcissist is going to start feeling depression, embarrassment, and shame.

One thing to note here is how a narcissist will often be the first to leave the relationship. Just when you have felt tired with the relationship, and like it isn't going anywhere, you will find that the narcissist is going to leave you first. This is often due to the fact that the narcissist is going to have a big fear of being abandoned. But they may be the one who decides to end that relationship because it allows them to feel like they are in control of the situation. But they still end up with the depression.

## Losing the narcissistic supply

Narcissists are going to survive off other people in order to fulfill their narcissistic supply. The emotional imbalance that occurs within this kind of person, such as the depression and the mood swings, are going to be linked to the fear of a loss of this supply. Whether they realize it or not, the narcissist is always worried that they won't be able to fill this need, that they won't be able to find others who are willing to give them the attention that they need. Even a small fluctuation in the amount of narcissistic supply can seem like a big deal, and it can end up with them having depression.

Once the narcissist starts to feel depressed, they may decide that it is time to socially withdraw from others. They don't want others to know about the depression because it can seem like a sign of weakness. But what this actually ends up doing is cutting the supply that they need down even more. This means that not only will the narcissist fall into a deep depression, but they will end up turning to their closest partner to get the attention and admiration that they need.

This can be a hard thing for that partner to work through. The narcissist, in an attempt to get the same amount of narcissistic supply from one person that they used to get out of many more, will start to become more belligerent towards their partner. And then the depression that comes with the narcissist will become a horrible and vicious spiral for themselves and for all of those around them.

Think about how alcoholics and drug addicts act. They are often going to have a lot of feelings of self-loathing. They know that they need the drink or the drug that they are addicted to and that they can't get by without it, but these addicts also hate that they are so dependent on this and that they don't have the right amount of strength in order to get away from the addiction.

It is believed by some that the narcissist is going to hate themselves because of their addiction to that narcissistic supply. Just as depression will come with the other forms of addiction, the addiction that the narcissist has to their narcissistic supply could cause them depression as well. When it shows up in the narcissist, it is going to be a form of depression that they don't like at all, and to others, they will act out with a lot of aggression and belligerence.

The lower this narcissistic supply becomes, the more depression the narcissist is going to feel. They need to have that steady supply of admiration from those around them. And if they had been used to getting it from a close partner for some time, it can definitely cause a level of depression in them when the partner finally decides that they have had enough and they want to leave.

Depression can be the result of criticism from someone who usually gives them only praise. People with NPD are going to hate criticism and will be sensitive, not only because it is going to upset the worldview that they have, the worldview of being perfect, but also because they may see that it could potentially become a total loss of their supply from that particular person. And the anxiety that they feel is going to lead the narcissist to feel depressed in the long run.

This is the interesting thing that can happen with the relationship. With normal and healthy relationships, the individual is going to feel sad because the relationship has ended. They spent a lot of time with that person, building memories, and building up life with them. Even if they were the ones who decided to break it off and move on, there can be a bit of depression because of the loss of the relationship.

But the narcissist is going to see this situation in a slightly different manner. They are not going to be concerned about losing the relationship because they lost the person, regardless of how long they were in that relationship. Instead, they are going to be upset because their narcissistic supply is gone. They aren't sure where they are going to get their admiration and attention from in the future, and this is what will lead to their depression.

At the most basic level here, depression can be a feeling of desperate and complete loneliness. Because the narcissist is going to lack empathy, they are going to lose their ability in order to connect with other people in their lives. Even with this lack of empathy, the narcissists are going to crave attention. Deep down though, they are going to be some of the loneliest people on earth, wanting empathy from others but unable to give it back to anyone else.

# Chapter 12: How to Handle Your Interactions with a Narcissist

Now that we have spent some time in this guidebook talking about narcissism and all of the different parts that come with it, it is time to take a look at how you should handle any interactions that you have with the narcissist in your life. There are many different places where you may encounter a narcissist. They may be your parent, your sibling, your aunt or uncle, your partner, your child, and even someone you work with. And with the instances of narcissism being so high and, on the rise, lately, you will find that it is more and more likely that you will need to interact with someone who has NPD.

Whether you need to stick with pleasantries or a light chat in the office hall, or you need to have a more serious talk with the person, you will need to change the way that you interact with the person who is dealing with NPD. Often, when you are talking to a person like this, you will find that the conversation isn't always going to come out the way that you want, think, or expect because of the way that the narcissist is going to handle it all. But when you have a better understanding of what you are able to expect from the narcissist, and you are able to handle them better, you will find that you can handle any narcissist who shows up in your life.

# How can I talk to someone who has NPD?

Normally, when you stop and have a discussion with another person, there is an expectation of the way that the other person is going to respond in general. But if they don't respond in the way that you were expecting, you may be visibly shocked by that. Often, the response that you are going to get from a narcissist is going to feel like a punch in the stomach because it takes you so off guard. It is very helpful to be prepared for these responses so that you are not taken off guard and can keep the conversation going.

When you talk to a narcissist, remember that it is best to never react with impatience, anger, or fear. There are some neutral responses that are the best to use in order to reduce the amount of intimidation or control that the narcissist is going to try and use on that conversation. For example, you may decide to keep your attitude curious or one of patience, and going with some responses or questions like "I'm not so clear about what that means. Can you please tell me more or clarify?"

On one hand, these questions allow you to put up the emotional boundary that is needed and helps you to not take the statements of the narcissist in a personal manner. You don't want to ever let them put you in the trap of feeling responsible or guilty, and you want to be able to maintain a bit of control over the situation. The narcissist is going to try and push back against any of the boundaries that you are trying to put up. But staying strong and keeping things pretty neutral rather than fighting back will make this much easier.

Now, there are going to be some times when you end up in a group situation with an individual who has NPD. You can still use the same kind of questions that we talked about above in order to make sure there is emotional space around you and to make the narcissist remain accountable for their statements. If you are at a loss for the types of questions and comments that you can make, whether you are alone with the narcissist or you are in a ground situation, practicing some of the following can make this easier:

- How did you come to that position or decision? What helped you to reach that position?
- What things did you consider before you made that decision? Can you help me out by making the intent of that statement clear?

In general, if you can, these pointers are going to help you to be deliberate and force the narcissist to come out with what they want. Sometimes, they are going to back off because they don't want to fall into a trap and look bad. And if they do come forward, they are going to have to give up their true positions, which makes it easier for you to walk away.

There are a lot of different things that you are able to do in order to engage with a narcissist, no matter how you know them. Some of these include:

1. Always listen to what they are saying carefully and think some thoughts that are pleasant. Even take the time to smile.
2. If the narcissist meets with you and sees you as a good source of support or a source of acknowledgment or recognition, then the communication is going to be easier to handle.

3. Try to add in some truthful recognitions and positive comments when you talk to the other person. You want to flatter them and make them feel good about talking with you, while still making sure that you are the one who is in control of the situation at all times. Never make the mistake of being insincere in flattering them because they will be able to see right through this.

4. Keep in mind that the narcissist not only doesn't like challenges or frustrations in their life, but they can't also handle it.

5. The narcissist is going to refuse to treat you as an equal to them, no matter what. Instead, they are probably going to have some unreasonable expectations of you, simply because, in their own minds, they are entitled to this.

# How can I stay strong and not let the narcissist manipulate me?

Many times, the person who has NPD is going to need to be in charge, to be the one who is right, and they always want to achieve their own agenda and goals. Because of this, it is their goal to work and manipulate the other person to help them reach these end goals. And since many narcissists are going to be very convincing and charming, it isn't too hard to see why the average person is going to get caught up in all of this and become manipulated.

It is important that you stay strong and hold your ground. If the narcissist is going to manipulate you, then this means that you are going to lose out in the long run because you won't have control over your life. The narcissist is not going to care how much they use you, as long as they are able to get what they want. There are three kinds of rules that you need to consider when you are trying to make sure that the narcissist doesn't manipulate you and these include:

1. Don't respond to any of their arguments. Instead, be a listener who is kind. If you find that they keep trying your patience and you are not able to just sit and listen, then find a way to leave the conversation.
2. Set a firm boundary with them, one that allows you to meet your own needs. You can warn the narcissist when they have pushed too far, and make it clear to them what is going to happen if they decide to infringe on this boundary.

3. If you find it necessary, leave the situation and find ways that you can take care of yourself with no guilt along the way.

Many times, someone who has NPD is going to try and take reality and twist and turn it so that none of the blame can be placed on them, and all of it is placed on you. They will often deny any fault at all, and you may be accused of being a liar, judgmental, unfair, or mean.

It is common for these narcissists to try and manipulate you if they think that you are criticizing them. First, they may start to feel anger and become defensive around you. Then they may make some demands that they expect you to meet. And if you fail or refuse to meet them, then they are going to be outraged at this. But if you decide to get angry with the narcissist in return, you may get to let out some of your feelings, but it doesn't provide you any protection from the manipulation in the future.

If you are in a close relationship with the narcissist, they could use finances in order to get you to act in a certain way. For example, the narcissist may decide to make you feel obligated to them or dependent on them through the finances. It is a good idea, especially at the beginning of the relationship, to have your own financial support so that you can never be manipulated by this.

The narcissist is going to be really good at getting under your skin. And there may be times when you have trouble dealing with the strong emotions or words of the narcissist. If this is true, it is a good idea to walk away and take a break. You can also work on developing a stronger self-confidence and self-esteem at the same time. Taking care of yourself and remembering that you do matter during this is going to be the best way that you can protect yourself from a narcissist.

## Can I get what I want from a narcissist?

When it comes to a significant other who is a narcissist, you may be able to get away and not have to deal with them any longer. But when it is a sibling, a parent, a child, or even a partner you have kids with, it may be hard to break off from them completely. And if you really love your job, but there is a narcissist who works there, you may not be able to escape from that either. This brings up the question, are you able to get what you want out of a narcissist or are you doomed to only ever do what they want?

If there is something that you would like to get out of the narcissist, whether it is them to help out with some chores or you would like to find a better way to deal with them, the biggest key is that you need to have a good understanding of how their mind works. When you know the way that this person is going to react and respond to you, then it becomes infinitely easier for you to know the right way to approach them.

First, always remember that the person who has NPD is going to want, need, and look for praise and admiration all of the time. The drive of the narcissist is going to be directed towards independence, influence, power, intelligence, or beauty. If you are able to figure out which one of these validation types that the narcissist likes the most, you can use it in some compliments to them. And once you give the compliment, make sure that they hear it before you proceed.

Basically, if you want to get something out of a narcissist, you need to show them how much they are able to benefit from it. Yes, they will need to do something small for you, but in the end, they are going to get something much more significant out of the deal. For example, let's say that you want to go to a movie, and you want the narcissist to agree to go with you. You know that this narcissist likes to talk about their superior intellect skills and that this is important to them. You may say something like, "The reviews all said this is not a film for the weak-minded; only the quickest minds will figure out the twists and turns" can get them to agree to go do what you want.

This all may seem a bit manipulative, but it is really what we do with all of the relationships. If we want to eat at a certain place with friends, we may use our influence to convince them. You just need to concentrate your efforts a bit more when it comes to the narcissist.

# How to stop being victimized or abused by the narcissist

Always remember that there should never be a time when you have feelings that you deserve anything less than respect. But because of some of the common behaviors that come with narcissism, it is possible that you could become a victim of abuse if you get into a relationship with a narcissist. Sometimes, this is mild verbal abuse, and sometimes, this goes a bit further and becomes physical abuse.

Being a victim of a circumstance or an incident should not make you feel ashamed. Always think about getting help if you end up in that situation, no matter how you got there. It is common for the narcissist to be charming, and to know exactly what to say to get you to be with them, to listen to them, and to take them in. And they may be able to hold up that façade for some time. But eventually, their true selves will come out, and you will be the victim left in the crossfire.

Work relationships, living relationships, and all other relationships are going to end up with some personality clashes at time. After the clash is done though, most people will find some healthy ways to resolve them and move on. But when the clash happens with a narcissist, it is almost impossible to resolve the clash. The narcissist is going to fight to be right, no matter whether they are actually right or not, and it can happen that you will become abused in the process. Never let this abuse slide or let it control you. There should always be a zero tolerance policy in all relationships, but especially with a narcissist, when it comes to abuse.

So, how are you supposed to avoid being a victim when you end up in a relationship with a narcissist? This can be hard. They often find a way to let themselves into your life, and all of a sudden, you have twirled around and living with them. But, as the novelty wears off and you start to learn more about them and their ways, you are going to be sucked in and may become a victim in this relationship with a narcissist. Some of the things that you can do to try and avoid this in your relationship include:

1. When you are communicating with a narcissist, whether it is over an argument or just a normal conversation, be prepared that their perception is going to be completely different from yours. And often, the narcissist is not going to consider the perceptions that you have.
2. You should always have a good support system behind you, including counselors, friends, and family so that you can still have some control over your life.
3. Have a life of your own. Often, narcissists want to make sure that they are able to be in control. They want to make sure that all of your attention is just on them and on nothing else. You can make sure that have your own life including financial independence, activities, hobbies, and work if possible to avoid complete isolation through the narcissist.
4. When you do communicate with this person, remember that you shouldn't take things too personally.
5. Make sure that you set up some realistic boundaries and then share them with the narcissist. Be ready to enforce these boundaries because it is likely that the narcissist is going to try and fight them

6. If you run into troubles where the narcissist becomes too demanding, you can use some topics like "I'm sorry you feel that way" or "Can I have a little breather to think about that?" can help you to get a buffer and think through decisions, rather than getting caught up in the moment.

The way that you interact with the narcissist is going to be quite a bit different compared to the way that you interact with others around you. They are not going to respond in the manner that you think they will, they will often demand things that are way unrealistic, and they may even become abusive if their actions are not checked, and if they are not given what they want. Being able to alter the way that you interact with a narcissist is going to make a big difference in whether you are able to maintain the control that you need over your own life.

# Conclusion

Thank you for making it through to the end. Let's hope it was informative and able to provide you with all of the tools you need to achieve your goals whatever they may be.

The next step is to start using some of the tips and tricks that are found in this guidebook when it comes to working with a narcissist or even getting treatment for someone who is already suffering from this condition. Many of us have come across a narcissist at some point in our lives, but very few know how to actually deal with this kind of person. This guidebook is going to give you the information and the tools that you need in order to do this.

Inside this guidebook, you are going to learn everything that you need to know about narcissistic personality disorder, or NPD, how to recognize the signs and symptoms of someone who has this condition, and even some of the best treatment options that you can use to help someone who has gone through this issue. Treatment is possible, and narcissists can start to learn how to change their way of thinking and talking, but it is something that takes time and it won't happen overnight.

Dealing with a narcissist in your life is never an easy experience. They are able to get full control over their victim, and they don't want to let go because this is the way that they get the focus and the attention that they want. Understanding the why behind all of this and learning the steps that you can take to change it around will make a big difference. Make sure to check out this guidebook to show you the exact steps that are needed to make this happen.

Finally, if you found this book useful in any way, a review on Amazon is always appreciated!

CPSIA information can be obtained
at www.ICGtesting.com
Printed in the USA
LVHW020720270521
688664LV00009B/989

9 781483 412146